I Like Computers

What Can I Be?

by Muriel L. Dubois

Consultant:
Barbara M. Parramore
Professor Emeritus, Curriculum and Instruction
North Carolina State University

Bridgestone Books
an imprint of Capstone Press
Mankato, Minnesota

Bridgestone Books are published by Capstone Press
151 Good Counsel Drive, P.O. Box 669, Mankato, Minnesota 56002
http://www.capstone-press.com

Library of Congress Cataloging-in-Publication Data
Dubois, Muriel L.
    I like computers: what can I be?/Muriel L. Dubois.
    p. cm.—(What can I be?)
    Includes bibliographical references and index.
    Summary: Simple text describes various careers for people who are interested in
computers, such as software designer, desktop publisher, computer animator, and
webmaster, and tells how to begin preparing for these careers.
    ISBN 0-7368-0631-8
    1. Computer science—Vocational guidance—Juvenile literature. [1. Computer science.
2. Occupations.] I. Title. II. Series.
QA76.25.D83 2001
004'.023'73—dc21   00-021354

Editorial Credits
Tom Adamson, editor; Heather Kindseth, designer; Katy Kudela, photo researcher

Photo Credits
Charles Gupton/Pictor, 8
David F. Clobes, 4
Gary Buss/FPG International LLC, cover
Index Stock Imagery, 12
International Stock/Patrick Ramsey, 10
Jack Glisson, 6
Kimberly Danger, 14, 20
Marilyn Moseley LaMantia, cover (top inset), 16
Philip Joseph/Pictor, cover (middle inset)
Pictor, cover (bottom inset)
Unicorn Stock Photos/Martin R. Jones, 18

1 2 3 4 5 6 06 05 04 03 02 01

Table of Contents

People Who Enjoy Computers. 5

Computer Technician 7

Software Designer. 9

Consultant 11

Graphic Artist 13

Desktop Publisher. 15

Webmaster 17

Computer Animator 19

Preparing to Work with Computers 21

Hands On: Searching the Internet 22

Words to Know 23

Read More 24

Internet Sites 24

Index. 24

People Who Enjoy Computers

You may like to use computers. You might like to solve math problems. Maybe you enjoy puzzles or thinking games. You might like to draw or paint. You can have a job working with computers when you grow up.

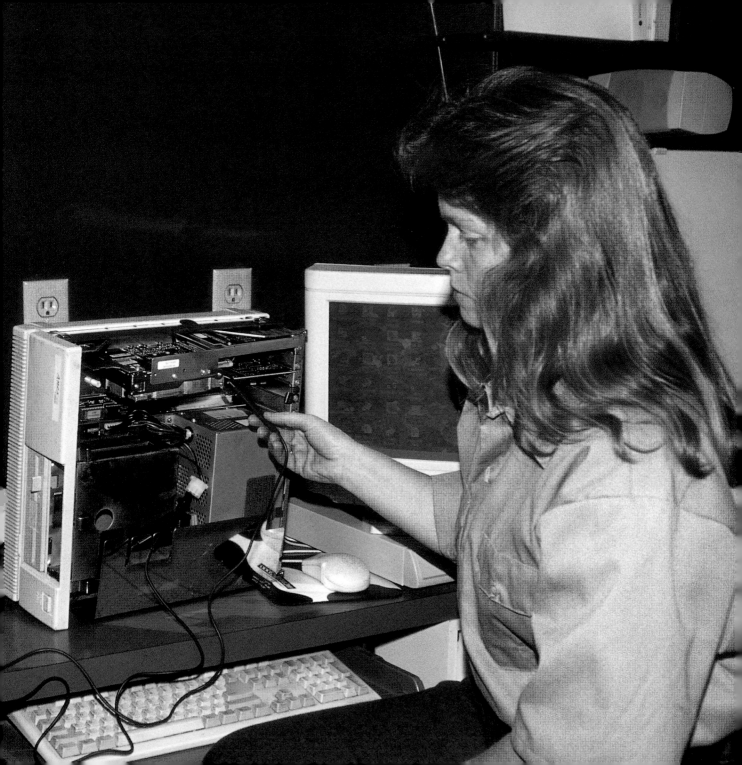

Computer Technician

Computer technicians build or fix computers. They work with computer hardware. Hardware includes the monitor, keyboard, and circuit board. Technicians fix computers at businesses or schools.

circuit board
a board with connected electronic parts that help the computer run

Software Designer

Software designers plan computer programs. A program tells the computer what to do. Designers enter instructions into a computer to make a program. Some programs help people do work. Other programs are games.

Consultant

Consultants are like teachers. They show people how computers work. Consultants help businesses choose the right computer and program for each job. Consultants teach people how to use software programs.

Graphic Artist

Graphic artists use computer programs to make designs with photographs, type, and drawings. These graphics can be used in books, movies, and advertisements. Graphic artists study both art and computers in school.

design
the shape or style
of something

13

Desktop Publisher

Desktop publishers use computers to make printed materials. They create books, magazines, or newspapers. They may work with writers and graphic artists. Desktop publishers use programs to arrange words and graphics on a page.

Webmaster

Webmasters plan sites for the World Wide Web. Web sites give information about people, places, businesses, and other subjects. Webmasters make sites easy to read and to use. They also keep sites up-to-date.

World Wide Web
a collection of Web sites that are part of the Internet

Computer Animator

Computer animators use software programs to make art that moves. Some computer animators create cartoons. Others add 3-D effects to movies or TV commercials. Computer animators also make video games.

3-D effects
three-dimensional effects; 3-D shapes are not flat.

Preparing to Work with Computers

You can prepare for a career in the computer field. Play computer games to see how graphics work. Use the Internet to learn more about computers. Your school or library may have computers you can use.

Hands On: Searching the Internet

The World Wide Web has many great sites for kids. Some of these sites can help you practice graphic arts or play video games. Others help you learn more about computer jobs. You can use the Internet Public Library to find these sites.

What You Need

A computer with Internet access

What You Do

1. Go to the Internet Public Library Web site. Enter the Web site's address: <http://www.ipl.org/youth>.
2. Click "Computers/Internet."
3. This area shows you how to find information about computers and searching the Internet.
4. You can search for almost anything that interests you at the Internet Public Library. Explore some of the other topics such as science, art and music, or fun stuff.

Words to Know

advertisement (ad-ver-TIZE-muhnt)—a notice that calls attention to a product or an event

consultant (kuhn-SUHL-tuhnt)—a person who teaches or gives advice to others

electronic (i-lek-TRON-ik)—powered by electricity; electricity is a form of energy.

Internet (IN-tur-net)—a connection of computer networks all around the world

monitor (MON-uh-tur)—a computer screen

program (PROH-gram)—a series of step-by-step instructions that tells a computer what to do

Read More

Raatma, Lucia. *Safety on the Internet*. Safety First! Mankato, Minn.: Bridgestone Books, 1999.

Reeves, Diane Lindsey, and Peter Kent. *Career Ideas for Kids Who Like Computers*. New York: Facts on File, 1998.

Sabbeth, Carol. *Crayons and Computers: Computer Art Activities for Kids Ages 4–8*. Chicago: Chicago Review Press, 1998.

Internet Sites

Awesome Library
http://www.awesomelibrary.com
BLS Career Information
http://stats.bls.gov/k12/html/edu_over.htm
Great Sites
http://www.ala.org/parentspage/greatsites/amazing.html

Index

art, 13, 19
businesses, 7, 11, 17
career, 21
designs, 13
games, 5, 9, 19, 21
graphics, 13, 15, 21
hardware, 7

Internet, 21
job, 5, 11
program, 9, 11, 13, 15, 19
school, 7, 13, 21
software, 9, 11, 19
Web sites, 17
World Wide Web, 17

004
Dub

Dubois, Muriel L.
I like computers :
what can I be ?

PERMA-BOUND.

DATE DUE			